Flags snapped in the breeze....

Horses stomped their feet. Gonzalo Pizarro swung his leg up over his horse. He rode down the long lines of those who were going with him. There were hundreds of men, and dogs, pigs, and even llamas.

Gonzalo galloped back to the head of the group. Everything was ready. He held his sword high. Onlookers cheered and shouted as the lines of men and animals began to move. They were sure that these searchers were the best ever. They would discover El Dorado, no doubt about it!

The most exciting, most inspiring, most unbelievable stories are the ones that really happened!

TOTALLY TRUE adventures!

THE SEARCH FOR
EL DORADO

Is the city of gold a real place?

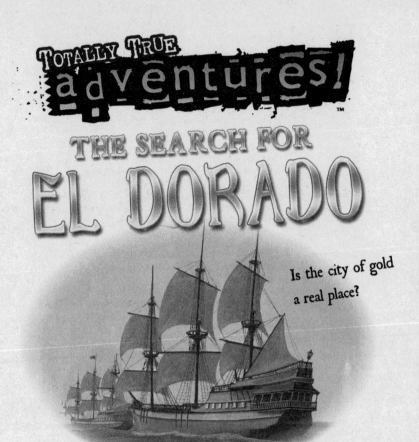

by Lois Miner Huey
illustrated by Wes Lowe

A STEPPING STONE BOOK™

Random House 🏠 New York

For Flynn, Ryan, and Ella:
may your lives be golden.

Text copyright © 2016 by Lois Miner Huey
Interior illustrations copyright © 2016 by Wesley Lowe

Visit us on the Web!
SteppingStonesBooks.com
randomhousekids.com

Educators and librarians, for a variety of teaching tools, visit us at
RHTeachersLibrarians.com

Library of Congress Cataloging-in-Publication Data
Huey, Lois Miner.
The search for El Dorado / by Lois Miner Huey ; illustrated by Wesley Lowe.
p. cm. — (Totally true adventures)
"A stepping stone book."
Audience: Ages 7–10.
ISBN 978-0-553-53614-0 (trade) — ISBN 978-0-553-53615-7 (lib. bdg.) —
ISBN 978-0-553-53616-4 (ebook)
1. America—Discovery and exploration—Juvenile literature. 2. El Dorado—
Juvenile literature. I. Lowe, Wesley, illustrator. II. Title.
E121.H82 2016 970.01—dc23 2015030320

Printed in the United States of America
10 9 8 7 6 5 4 3 2 1

This book has been officially leveled by using the F&P Text Level
Gradient™ Leveling System.

Random House Children's Books supports the First Amendment
and celebrates the right to read.

CONTENTS

HOW IT BEGAN

A legend is a powerful story. It is a tale about important people and their adventures. Each one has a little bit of truth, but also a little bit of make-believe. Some are known by only a small group. Some are known by many people. The legend of El Dorado spread around the world, and it changed many lives. But it all started with a story like this. . . .

Long ago, a young man stood in the morning sun next to a large lake. He had strong muscles in his chest, arms, and legs. This was a body fit for a chief.

So why were men smearing mud all over it?

The old chief of the Muisca tribe had died. The men sprinkled gold dust on the young man's body from the bottom of his feet to the top of his head. The gold stuck to the mud and glowed in the sun. Now he was the Golden Man.

Would the great god of the lake accept this young man as the next leader?

The Golden Man sat on a raft made of reeds as he was rowed across the smooth surface of the water. People standing onshore and on the hills cheered. The sound echoed all around. The god of the lake surely would hear it.

The Golden Man threw jewels into the middle of the lake. These sank. They were gifts to the god.

The Golden Man took a deep breath. Then he dove into the cold water. He went down, down, down to where the god lived. The gold dust on his body spread across the water in a shiny cloud. It slowly sank, too. Would the god be pleased?

The man came back up. He swam to shore. He pulled himself out of the water. The mud and gold were gone. The god had accepted him!

The crowds cheered even louder. The young man smiled at them all.

The Golden Man was now chief.

This was the story of "El Dorado," the Golden Man. The tale was told again and again, and it became a legend. Some of it may have happened—but maybe not all of it!

CHAPTER
I

THE AMERICAS

Legends can come from anywhere, and the legend of El Dorado began in South America. South America is a large continent with many different climates. It can be a beautiful and dangerous place. On the west coast, the tall Andes Mountains are very difficult to climb. Below the mountains, the jungles are hot and steamy. The plants here are thick and tough, and it is almost impossible to find a path. The Amazon River flows through this rain forest. It starts in the Andes Mountains and goes all the way to the Atlantic Ocean. It is one of the longest rivers in the world. It is so wide that in some places you can't see across it. This can make it hard to travel along the river.

Centuries ago, many native people lived in South America. Most lived in small villages ruled by chiefs. These natives had not invented the wheel or written languages. They had no farm animals, like cows or horses. Instead, they had woolly animals called llamas. Sometimes different groups fought, but they didn't use guns. Their warriors had spears and arrows.

One of these tribes was called the Muisca. They had a special way to choose a new leader: the Golden Man ceremony.

We're not sure how many people belonged to this tribe. Their small villages were spread out in the mountains of what is now Colombia and part of Venezuela. They did almost no hunting. Instead, they grew crops like corn, potatoes, squash, and beans on flat land cut out of hillsides. They even invented calendars to keep track of farming seasons.

Muisca villages were filled with round homes made of clay. They had roofs of wood and straw, with small doors and windows in the walls. The Muisca were experts at making clay pots. They painted the pots and cut lines into the clay to decorate them. They also wove cotton cloth and made jewelry like necklaces, bracelets, and nose rings. The

favorite material for their metal crafts was gold. They learned to melt it and mix it with copper to make it stronger. The Muisca were famous for this discovery.

The Muisca were great traders. They brought in fish, fruit, and honey from other parts of South America. Their homes in high land protected them from enemies. If they were threatened, they could come together under the leadership of their chief.

At this time, people in South America used about a thousand different languages. Traders learned the languages of other groups or used their hands to talk. They loved to tell each other stories. As the Muisca traveled for trade, they proudly told the tale of their Golden Man ceremony. The story changed as it spread from person to person and language to language. Some stories said the ceremony was a small one. Others said there were large crowds watching. Over time, it grew from one Golden Man . . . to a large golden city.

———————◆◆◆———————

Years passed. After a while, the Muisca no longer covered someone with gold when it was time to choose a new leader. But they all knew the story of what their ancestors had done.

Then one day, in the 1500s, the chiefs of the Muisca tribes came together. They crowded into the head chief's large round house with its golden doors. They had traveled from their villages to hear what he had to say.

People sat on the floor on woven mats while the head chief spoke. He told them he'd heard stories of strange men who had appeared in their land. These strangers wore hard gray metal over their chests and heads. They rode big four-legged animals. The village chiefs didn't know what to think. They had no idea who these new people were. Maybe they were gods? The chiefs returned to their villages. They still wondered what this meant. Where had these strangers come from? And why were they here?

The people of North and South America

had discovered this land thousands of years ago. Now another group of men had found it. They were from Europe. Once they had arrived, many changes were coming.

CHAPTER 2

COLUMBUS AND GOLD

In South America, many people had learned the story of a Golden City. Soon stories about South American gold would also become famous in Europe.

In the 1400s and 1500s, Europe was very different than it is today. It was a group of countries ruled by kings and queens. They had knights on horseback and powerful armies to help them take over more land. Kings and queens, nobles, and church men needed to show everyone that they were in charge. A

great way to do that was to show off how rich they were. The most important people in Europe wore shiny treasures like heavy gold chains with glittering jewels. If you had gold, it meant that you had power.

Important buildings in Europe were decorated with gold, too. Most people lived in simple wooden houses or huts. Churches were very different. Inside, altars gleamed with gold and silver. Beautiful pictures of saints looked down from ceilings, walls, and posts. Artists even used thin layers of gold in their paintings. Stained-glass windows let some sunlight in, but only a little. Instead, tall glowing candles in gold holders helped light the room. When people saw the riches inside these churches, they knew that they were in a special place.

Much of this gold came from far away.

Europeans traveled to Asia and the Middle East over long roads so they could buy and trade for spices, gold, and more. Then things changed. By 1492, these roads had to close because of war. It became harder for Europeans to get riches. Even so, they were hungry for more.

One man thought he had an answer. His name was Christopher Columbus. Columbus was an Italian sailor. He believed he could find a new way to get from Europe to Asia. He would sail west across the Atlantic Ocean until he got to Asia.

Columbus was born in 1451 in northern Italy. As a boy, he loved ships. He went to sea as a teenager and sailed on the Mediterranean and Aegean Seas. Life on the water could be very dangerous. When he was on a ship in the Atlantic Ocean, it was attacked by pirates.

His ship was burned, and Columbus had to swim to the shore. He arrived in a country called Portugal. From there, he went to the capital city. He married and had a son. When his wife died, Columbus took his son, Diego, to Spain. He worked on Spanish ships, mostly sailing to Africa.

At this time, explorers didn't know much about the geography of the world. Many educated people knew that the Earth was round. But were there any lands between Europe and Asia? Was it possible to sail across the ocean? Nobody could say. Many thought that sailing across the Atlantic Ocean was too dangerous. Still, Columbus liked the idea of reaching Asia by water. Once he got there, he could load up a ship with gold, silver, and spices and return a very rich man. (He didn't know, of course, that two continents stood in his way.)

Columbus had a plan but no money. He tried to get the king of Portugal and leaders in Italy to help. If they paid him, he could carry out his plan. They all said no. So he returned to Spain. With his friends, he asked the king and queen there to help him. This took a long time. The king and queen weren't sure Columbus knew what he was talking about, but they did listen. Finally, they agreed to pay just enough for three small ships.

In August 1492, Columbus set off across the Atlantic Ocean. He arrived on an island in the Caribbean on October 12. It looked like his belief had paid off. He was going to be rich!

On this first trip, Columbus met some of the island's natives. He saw that they were wearing gold. He traded for it by giving them glass beads, cloth, and tiny brass bells. The chief gave him a large mask with pieces of gold in the ears and eyes. Then Columbus sent some of his men into the middle of the island. When they came back, they said they had seen big piles of gold. They were lying, but Columbus believed every word.

Columbus sailed back to Spain. He promised the king and queen that he would give them as much gold as they want. He then wrote a letter about all the gold in the lands he visited. The letter was read all over Europe, and gold fever spread.

Now Columbus had to deliver lots of gold or lose the king and queen's support. He wrote in a different letter that "Gold is a wonderful thing! Whoever owns it is lord of all he wants." He knew that getting more gold would give him more power. But he did not find much during his next three trips. He lost royal help and died a poor and sick man in 1506.

Columbus never told any stories about a city made of gold. But his letter sent many gold seekers across the ocean. Soon they heard the legend of the hidden city called El Dorado. *Dorado* means "golden" in Spanish. And some explorers really did find gold. A soldier named Hernán Cortés found treasure in Mexico. Another named Francisco Pizarro found huge amounts of gold and silver in Peru. He melted the metal into bars and sent them home.

Europeans had found some of the riches they hoped for. But there were big problems. With this much gold around, people just wanted more. Shops and traders raised prices for their goods. Up and up and up the prices went. This made some people richer, but most people became poorer. Many of these poor people sailed to the Americas. It was a "New World" where they could find gold, too.

Many people suffered greatly along the way. Wooden ships were easily destroyed by storms. Going up and down on huge ocean waves made people very sick, and many died. Food rotted and was full of bugs. Captains treated people badly to make everyone behave. Most of those who lived through these terrible months on the seas did not find gold. Some settled down to farm land in the New World. Many returned home sick and poorer, wishing they hadn't gone.

Why would people go through all this just to find gold?

They went to be rich. They believed gold could be found without much work. The truth is that gold doesn't lie on top of the ground. It's rare, and when found, it's very hard to get. This is one reason why gold is worth a lot of money.

It was exciting to think about gold in places like El Dorado, where it would be easy to find. The stories said that gold could be picked up off shining streets. You could break it off roofs on buildings or pick it from trees. Glittering golden birds, animals, and fish could be captured. It was piled up inside buildings waiting to be found. Wow! People's imaginations went wild, and the stories got even bigger.

But where *was* El Dorado?

CHAPTER
3

THE SPANISH SEARCH

The Spanish saw gold as wealth. It was worth money, and it was a way to become powerful. But to the natives of South America, gold was more than wealth. They believed it contained pieces of the sun, and they weren't willing to give it up. If the Europeans wanted it, they had to take it from them by force. And that is exactly what happened. The newcomers stole the gold. They made slaves of the natives and forced them to mine it.

The Europeans wanted to keep looking

in new places. Since so much treasure had been found in Peru and Mexico, surely there would be even more in the middle of South America. That had to be where El Dorado was located. The Spanish set out to find it. One of those Spanish explorers was named Gonzalo Pizarro. Once he arrived in South America, it seemed like the perfect place for him to find treasure.

It was 1541, nearly fifty years since Columbus's searches. On the first day of his adventure, Gonzalo got ready to explore this new world. He swung his leg up over his horse. Flags snapped in the breeze. Horses stomped their feet. Gonzalo was sure he was going to find the golden city. Some Spanish explorers had already tried to find El Dorado, but Gonzalo had more money than any of them.

Gonzalo ordered his 200 soldiers up onto their horses. Then he continued along row after row of native slaves. Most of them were from what is now Peru. Next, he looked over the group's food. They were taking along

thousands of pigs to eat. A crowd of barking dogs would help them hunt other meat. Finally, in the back were the llamas. These animals had long necks and could carry supplies on their backs.

Gonzalo galloped back to the head of the line. His men were ready. Gonzalo held his sword high. Onlookers cheered and shouted as the group began to move. They were sure that these searchers would discover El Dorado, no doubt about it.

Gonzalo and his troop struggled through the high, cold Andes Mountains. They had to go up and around many large rocks. Next, they came down into the hot, thick rain forest. The men had to slash their way through branches and vines. It was a tiring way to get anywhere. They looked down to avoid poisonous snakes and up into the trees for jaguars. The native slaves often ran away. This meant the soldiers had to do more work. Pigs also escaped, which meant less food. Even for the best explorers, this was a dangerous place.

As they traveled, they met many new tribes of natives. The natives realized that the Spanish wanted gold. Instead of attacking them, they tricked them. They told them that El Dorado was real. If they just kept going a few more miles, they'd find it. In this way, the natives sent the Spanish away from their villages. They knew El Dorado was not really nearby, of course. But they could see that the Europeans greed would keep them going. The natives were right! The Spanish soldiers pushed on into the jungle.

El Dorado never appeared. The soldiers ate all the pigs, and next would be the dogs, llamas, and horses. The food ran low. Gonzalo sent a trusted friend named Francisco de Orellana to look for food.

Steady rain fell. The men were hungry and sick, but there was no sign of Francisco.

Gonzalo realized after a few weeks that Francisco wasn't coming back. Gonzalo turned for home. He had left Peru with a big group of men and animals. He came back a year later with only a few men left.

———◆◆▶———

Meanwhile, Francisco de Orellana had his own adventure. He took his men over 2,000 miles down the great Amazon River. They drew maps and wrote notes about what they saw. They met many people who promised them there was a lot of food and gold just ahead. Later, the men said they were attacked by women with bows and arrows. Their arrows went so deep into the Spanish boats that they looked like porcupines. One man in the Spanish group said that the women were tall and strong and had long braided hair that they

wrapped around their heads. They reminded him of an old Greek myth about powerful women called Amazons. He called these South American women Amazons, too.

Finally, Francisco and his men reached the end of the Amazon River. They had arrived at the Atlantic Ocean. They took a ship back to Spain to report their discoveries. They told stories of great riches, even though they hadn't found any. And they described beautiful women warriors. The women became another South American legend. The Amazon River is named after them.

———◆◆◆———

Two other Spanish groups came to explore, and they thought they had found a clue to El Dorado. They came across a lake that could have been where the Golden Man threw

treasure. It looked just like it was described in the stories. They tried taking water out of the lake, in case there was gold at the bottom.

Slaves went to work. They stood in a long line. They filled a bucket, passed it down the line, and poured the water on land. They did this for three months! They got the lake lower by about nine feet but found only a little gold. They gave up.

Later, a businessman tried. He had workmen dig a ditch across the edge of the lake. Sixty feet of water flowed out of the lake. Some gold jewelry was found. But the work was too dangerous to continue.

The Spanish never found El Dorado. But while they looked, much of South America was discovered and mapped. The strong belief in this legend opened up South America for other people. Families came from Spain, the Netherlands, and Portugal to settle this land. Except for Brazil, where Portuguese is spoken, all South American countries speak Spanish today.

The search for El Dorado didn't happen only in South America. Europeans looked for gold in North America, too. There, the legend had grown even bigger. It had become at least seven cities of gold!

CHAPTER
4

THE SEVEN CITIES OF GOLD

By 1539, the search for the Seven Cities of Gold was under way. One of those searches was happening close to a city called Cibola, in what is now New Mexico. A man named Father Marcos de Niza quietly climbed a hill that overlooked the city. Father Marcos didn't dare take his men there. He was afraid of being attacked. But he believed in the legend of the Seven Cities of Gold and wanted to see

if this was one of them. If it was, he would become a very rich man.

As he reached the top of the hill, he smiled. The city glowed in the early-morning sun. It had buildings built of stone as high as four stories. Gold and shiny blue stone decorated the walls and windows. He was sure he had found one of the golden cities.

Why was he so sure? Because in North America, two legends had joined together. People in Europe had heard stories about seven cities of gold, but no one knew where they were. Once the Americas were discovered, mapmakers began making more guesses. They marked the seven cities on different places on maps. The Spanish came to North America with these maps. They had a feeling that the seven cities of gold were there somewhere. Then they heard the legend of

El Dorado from the natives. That made true believers out of them. The seven golden cities must be real. They had to be found!

Before Father Marcos left, he piled stones up into a mound and placed a cross on top. This meant he was claiming all seven cities for the Spanish king. When he returned to Mexico City, his story got many people excited. Men from all around begged to go next. The Spanish leader in Mexico City decided another group should go. He put his friend Francisco Vázquez de Coronado in charge.

Coronado had been born in Spain to a rich family. But the family's money went to his older brother. Coronado needed to find his own way. He heard tales of gold in the New World. He went to Mexico City and was soon a favorite leader there. He became governor of an area next to the Pacific Ocean in

Mexico. In his new home, he enjoyed swimming in the sea and eating good food. But he never stopped wanting to find gold. When it was time to start a new search, he jumped at the chance.

Father Marcos went on the trip as a guide for Coronado. He had traveled through river valleys and a stretch of desert during his earlier trip. Coronado had only spent time in the cooler parts of Mexico. He wasn't ready for the large deserts, deep canyons, and flat grassy plains of North America.

Francisco de Coronado set out in February 1540. He rode on a horse wearing shiny golden armor so it was clear he was in charge. He was leading about 300 men on strong horses. Soldiers carrying spears and muskets stood ready. Priests in brown robes stood with them. They planned to bring Christianity

to the natives. Several hundred natives also went with him. They had red and black designs painted on their bodies and wore headdresses made of parrot feathers. They held bows and arrows while they waited for Coronado's command to march. Thousands of cattle, sheep, and pigs followed.

Coronado and his men reached Cibola, the town Father Marcos had discovered. They found buildings made of stone and clay bricks, but no gold. No shiny blue stone. Just a small town.

Had Father Marcos lied? Historians are not sure. Some think he did. Or some think the sunlight struck the town so it looked like it glowed with gold.

Coronado's men treated Marcos badly after that. He decided he wasn't safe, so he returned to Mexico City. But Coronado and his men still believed the seven cities were out there somewhere. They continued to look for it-for two more years!

For the first year, they went north. The land they searched is now Arizona and New Mexico. There were no golden cities. Then a native told Coronado about a golden city in what is now Texas. No luck there, either. *Then* they heard about a city in what is now Kansas. It turned out to be a village of tepees.

The clues did not lead to treasure, but Coronado found plenty of amazing new things. Before this trip, Europeans did not know about the Great Plains in the middle of North America. The Spanish were very surprised by it. They walked through tall grass, but when they looked back, the grass had sprung right back into place. The men couldn't tell where they had been just minutes

before. They couldn't mark their trail for others to follow or find their way back. They had never seen such a grassy place!

Hailstorms, snow, and frozen rivers made their trip harder. One time, snow fell all night. It covered the supplies and the soldiers, and even half buried the horses. This was only one of many storms they had to suffer through. They looked for warm, dry

places to sleep, but all of the villages were hard to reach.

In the end, Coronado only had a hundred men left. He returned to Mexico City. He took a shortcut that the natives showed him. This path became the Santa Fe Trail. Later on, it would be used by wagon trains going west across North America.

After two years, Coronado had gone

through the states of Arizona, New Mexico, Texas, Oklahoma, and Kansas. He and his men thought they were failures. They had not found treasure. They had starved, camped in small, cold dwellings, run out of water, and been bitten by snakes. They'd seen the Great Plains, "cows with humps" (which we call bison), and bighorn sheep. They had met many different native groups, from the Pueblos in their clay brick towns to the Wichita who lived in lodges made of grass and tepees.

Some of Coronado's men saw the Grand Canyon. The sight was a wonder to them all. It was truly something "grand." A canyon is a deep valley. It has been carved by a river flowing through it for millions of years. Coronado's men peered down from the edge

and saw its bottom. It was more than a mile down. The rock layers were many different colors, like red, gray, black, and brown.

Three of the men tried to climb down to the bottom. It had seemed like an easy job at the top of the canyon, but it turned out to be very difficult. They quickly found out the rocks were larger than they looked. Each layer of rock was over 275 feet tall. The men didn't get far. After they reached about one-third of the way down, they gave up. When they asked their native guides how far the canyon stretched, they said it went on for-ever. (It's actually 277 miles long.)

Explorers in the New World nearly always found something amazing. The Grand Canyon was the biggest wonder of them all. When they found these special sights, they claimed the land for Spain. No other European country tried to take over the American Southwest for hundreds of years.

The explorers didn't know it, but they had a huge effect on some native groups. Until then, natives on the Great Plains were farmers. They hunted on foot and used dogs to pull loads. Then some horses escaped their Spanish owners, and some were captured. These horses changed the natives' way of life.

Soon native people raised horses in America. They bought and sold them among themselves. They rode them into battle. They used them for carrying loads and for bison hunting. Now they could move quickly across the plains. They could bring down huge bison with their spears and arrows. Bison had always been a part of their diets, but after the

introduction of horses, it became the center of their lives. Bison provided meat, and the hides, horns, and bones were used for clothing, blankets, teepee coverings, and tools.

The legend of El Dorado and the Seven Cities of Gold story came together in Mexico and the southwestern United States. These legends promised gold, but once again, it was a dream that never really came true. Instead, the legend led to big parts of North America being mapped. This also meant that much of the continent was ruled by the Spanish. The Southwest still has signs of Spanish ownership. Cities like El Paso, Santa Fe, San Diego, Los Angeles, and San Francisco have Spanish names. Hundreds of years later, the southwestern states and California became part of the United States. This area brought many Spanish foods, clothing, and holiday celebrations to the country.

During this same time period, English explorers were sailing the oceans, too. They also wanted gold and glory. The story of El Dorado first belonged to the natives of South America. Then it became a Spanish story. And the legend kept spreading. It wasn't long before El Dorado was talked about by the English. Now it was their turn to search for the world's biggest treasure.

CHAPTER 5

SIR WALTER RALEIGH

People in England already had their own legends and stories. For example, there was a famous tale about Queen Elizabeth and how she met one of her best friends. The story went something like this. . . .

One day, in 1582, the English royal court was full of well-dressed young men and women. They watched as Queen Elizabeth walked toward them. She had red hair, nice clothes, and beautiful jewels. Suddenly the queen stopped. There was a big wet spot on the ground. A queen should not have to get her dress dirty! Handsome Walter Raleigh rushed to help her. He threw his fancy new cape on the ground. The queen crossed over, and her dress was saved. After that, Walter was one of her favorites.

Did this really happen? Perhaps. The story was printed in 1662, so it may be true . . . or not. Either way, it shows the kind of person Walter Raleigh was. He was clever and brave, and he would do anything to get the queen's attention. For many years, he was one of her closest friends.

Queen Elizabeth I is said to be one of the best rulers England ever had. During her time, great writers made poems and plays for her. One of them was the famous William Shakespeare. Elizabeth was also a powerful queen. Her sailors went all over the world to claim land for England.

She also had a big enemy: Spain. The Spanish didn't want Elizabeth to be queen of England, or any country. England and Spain were at war for many years. In 1588, Spanish ships even came to attack England. But the English were lucky. Bad weather helped them destroy the Spanish ships. Elizabeth was still queen. Walter won battles against Spain, so Elizabeth made him a knight. He became Sir Walter Raleigh.

But Sir Walter made a mistake. He secretly married one of Elizabeth's companions without her permission. She was very angry with him, and he needed to win her friendship again. If he helped her win more land and riches, maybe she would forgive him.

Could he claim more land for her in the Americas? Sir Walter had already tried to start a colony in North America for English settlers. In the 1580s, he settled a colony called Roanoke in what is now North Carolina. Then the colony suddenly disappeared. Even

now, no one knows where those people went or what happened to them. The story of the Lost Colony is still an American legend.

Sir Walter had failed once in North America. He did not want to fail again. Now he had a new idea. Instead of starting a colony, he could search for El Dorado. He wanted "to seek new worlds for gold, for praise, for glory." For years, Spanish ships had come back to Europe with treasure. Sir Walter planned to go into Spanish South America himself. He could take the gold right from the land.

In 1595, Sir Walter led a large group of ships to hunt for El Dorado. He would also spy on the Spanish in South America. Sir Walter knew they had treated the natives terribly, and he had an idea. He ordered his men not to take even a pineapple or potato from the natives without paying them.

The natives welcomed him when he told them he was an enemy of Spain. They gave his men shelter and sold them food. But they also knew that Sir Walter only wanted their gold. They had already led Spanish explorers on a wild-goose chase. They would do the same with the English. El Dorado was just ahead, they said. They told Sir Walter about a rich gold mine in the mountains, too. Then natives said there was a whole land full of gold nearby. All he had to do was cross over some high mountains. But Sir Walter knew he couldn't go on. He wasn't ready to hike over mountains. He promised the natives he would be back, and he sailed home to England.

Once he was home, he spread stories about finding a golden land. He hoped others would give him money so he could take many more men back there. But the queen didn't believe him. Many others thought he was lying, too. The El Dorado story had been around for years. People were losing hope that the legend was real.

In 1603, Queen Elizabeth I died. The new king, James I, didn't like Sir Walter. Sir Walter had been loyal to the queen. James was afraid that Queen Elizabeth's friends might try to take away his power. He even threw Sir Walter in jail for not being loyal to the king. Sir Walter was popular with the English people. The king was too scared to hurt him. But he kept him in jail for thirteen years! Sir Walter spent his time writing poems and a book about the history of the world.

Then Sir Walter's luck seemed to change. By 1614, King James needed money. Sir Walter told the king that he could bring back gold from South America. The king freed him from jail in 1616 and agreed to the plan. However, Sir Walter had to make a few promises. He could not attack the Spanish.

James didn't want another war with Spain. He couldn't afford it! And Sir Walter had to return with gold—or else.

Sir Walter knew it would be very hard to stay clear of the Spanish. They wouldn't want the English there. If they found him, they would fight him. But he was sure he would find lots of shiny gold. Then the king would forgive him no matter what happened.

Almost everything went wrong during Sir Walter's second search. Wild storms slowed the ships. Fever broke out on board. Sir Walter was in his sixties, and he became very ill. Finally, the ships landed in Trinidad. It was an island just off the coast of South America. Sir Walter was too sick to go into the jungle.

Instead, he sent some of his men to find

the gold. One of them was his son, Wat. He also put his friend Lawrence Kemys in charge. Lawrence had been with Sir Walter on the first trip. Lawrence said he knew where the gold was, but he didn't. They never found very much treasure. Even worse, Wat got into trouble. He was a young man and didn't always think about his actions. He attacked a Spanish fort and was killed.

Sir Walter returned to England an old man. He was tired, sick, and sad about the loss of his son. He held just two nuggets of gold. The king was angry, of course. Sir Walter had not kept his promises. This was the perfect excuse to finally get rid of Sir Walter. The king ordered for him to be killed in 1618.

◆◆▶

Once again, belief in El Dorado made men seek gold. Once again, they failed. The legend was more of a nightmare than a dream. After Sir Walter's trips, the English no longer believed in it. Instead, they worked on bringing people to North America. They came to grow their businesses, or to freely practice their religion, or to start a new life. But this was not easy. There were mountain lions, bears, wolves, and poisonous snakes. The native

people realized the Europeans wanted to take their land. That made them dangerous enemies. The weather could also be harsh, with deep snows, wild winds, and terrible heat. All in all, North America was not a safe place.

Still, small groups of settlers tried. A colony called Jamestown was started in Virginia in 1609. It came very close to failing. Luckily, a ship full of supplies came just in time. The settlers kept going and made the place

a success. A group of religious settlers, the Pilgrims, sailed across the ocean on a ship called the *Mayflower*. The Puritans, another religious group, settled nearby. They called this area New England. Later, Quakers settled Pennsylvania. By 1664, the English had taken over colonies in New York, New Jersey, and Delaware. And a little more than a hundred years later, in 1776, the Declaration of Independence was written. It called for a "United States of America."

CHAPTER 6

THE GOLDEN MOUNTAIN

For hundreds of years, the dream of gold brought big changes to the Americas. It even helped bring about the United States of America. But the legend of El Dorado wasn't done yet.

Mud Springs was a town in California. It changed its name to El Dorado in the 1850s. Why? Gold had been discovered there. Men hurried west by wagon or by ship to get

some. This time it was called a gold rush, and Mud Springs became a center for the search. Americans remembered the El Dorado story, so they borrowed that name for their booming town. A few did get rich. Most did not. In fact, the people who made the most money were those who sold mining tools to the gold-crazy newcomers!

Thanks to the greed for gold, California was settled quickly. During the 1800s, the land between the east and west coasts was settled, too. There were other rushes when silver and gold were found in states like Montana and Alaska. Mostly people wanted land. But even in the early 1900s, some people still believed that El Dorado was real. One of them was an airplane pilot named Jimmie Angel.

Jimmie was born in Missouri in 1899. He

was tall with black hair and brown eyes. His face was covered with scars from a fire in one of his airplanes. Jimmie flew planes during World War I. After the war, he showed off his great flying skills for people who would pay to watch. He was known as a daredevil pilot. He would do brave stunts and would fly anywhere.

Soon he began making trips to South America. A country called Venezuela was his favorite place. In the 1900s, South America had many cities, ranches, and mines. Europeans from Spain, Portugal, and Germany had settled there. Many families had mothers and fathers from different backgrounds. Before the time of Christopher Columbus, people in Europe and the Americas didn't know very much about each other. Exploration had changed that.

But some parts of South America had still hidden secrets.

In Venezuela, Jimmie heard the legend of El Dorado. The story had changed again. Now it was not a city or country–it was a golden mountain! The story made Jimmie dream of exciting adventure. Since Jimmie was a pilot, he decided to look for El Dorado from the air.

About that time, Jimmie said he met a man who made him a strange offer. The man paid him $5,000 to fly him to a mysterious place in Venezuela. Jimmie had never been there before. Jimmie said that after they landed the plane, something amazing happened. He watched the man walk to a nearby river and collect many pounds of gold. Surely, Jimmie thought, this must be El Dorado.

No one knows if this story was true. Jimmie told it so many times that it became a legend, too. Jimmie spent many years trying to get people to help him look for this golden mountain again.

In 1933, Jimmie made the flight that changed his life. It was in the same area where he believed he'd seen the golden mountain. When he looked out the window, he saw heavy clouds sitting over the thick jungle. He flew his plane closer. In a hole in the mist, he saw a very tall waterfall tumbling off a mountain. The water fell for so long in the hot air that it was turning into a thick mist. He was sure the waterfall was a mile high! It was so beautiful that it took his breath away.

But the giant waterfall wasn't on any of his maps. Later, he told others about this waterfall, and they laughed at him. If it was real,

why had no one else ever seen it? Finally, in 1935, Jimmie flew back to the waterfall with a group of men. They gasped when they saw it going down the tall mountain. Jimmie repeated his story about the gold. If they landed, he was sure they would find treasure. None of the men wanted to land the plane. But after that, nobody could call Jimmie Angel a liar. People began to call the waterfall Angel Falls after him.

How could such a large waterfall not be on any maps? Why didn't people know about it? Of course, the natives had known for thousands of years. The falls are wrapped in mist most of the time, so few Europeans had seen it. It is possible that one famous European did—Sir Walter Raleigh! Sir Walter had been there hundreds of years earlier. And he had believed a golden city was there, too. Had

Raleigh seen the falls? Probably not. But it is possible. Both men explored the same area. Both men said they knew there was treasure there.

———— ◆·▸ ————

Two years later, Jimmie landed his plane on a flat area on top of the mountain. The ground was too soft to hold up the plane. The wheels sank in, and the airplane's nose fell deep into mud. The three people with him climbed out. They spent two days searching for gold but found nothing. The plane was too broken to fly again. They were going to have to leave it there and hike out. Jimmie didn't want the plane to sit with its nose like that, so they used ropes to pull up the nose. They tore cloth to make the letters ALL OK and an arrow to show which way they were going. They taped

the cloth message to a wing and left.

Rescue planes tried to find them, but low clouds and the mist hid the plane and Jimmie's group. Everyone thought they were lost or dead. But eleven days later, they walked out of the wilderness.

The El Dorado legend was still nowhere to be found. When people looked for the lost city, they seemed to find more trouble than gold. But some good came out of it. Everyone thought all the wonders of South America had been found. Then Jimmie Angel proved there were still surprises–like a huge waterfall. It had been unknown to Europeans for hundreds of years, but it was there all along. Maybe there are other places yet to be found and explored!

———— ◆ ◆ ▶ ————

Jimmie and his passengers said they saw strange plants and animals at the top of the mountain. They said it was like a lost world. Museums sent scientists to study this place. They discovered new kinds of snakes, birds, and plants on the mountain. Experts also measured the height of the waterfall. It was the tallest in the world!

Angel Falls is now one of the most popular places to visit in Venezuela. People get there

by river. Early one morning, a visitor noticed something strange: "We saw what looked like 'liquid gold flowing off the falls' in the sunlight. I said to myself, this must have been El Dorado." Even though this mountain isn't El Dorado, some people do see "gold" in Angel Falls.

Jimmie's plane sat on top of the mountain for thirty-three years. Finally, in 1964, the plane became a national treasure. It was taken apart in 1970, and a helicopter took the pieces to a museum. It was put back together and is now on display.

Jimmie Angel didn't find gold. But the world's tallest waterfall is named after him. He discovered a new place for scientists and tourists to explore. And his plane was declared a treasure!

CHAPTER
7

THE POWER OF LEGENDS

Legends are based on a small bit of truth. Myths are not. For example, Greek myths are stories about gods who never really existed. The legend of El Dorado is based on the story of the Golden Man. The Muisca people really did have a ceremony to pick their leader.

For people who believe, both myths and legends have their own power. Have you ever played Gossip or Telephone? In this game, people stand or sit in a line or circle. One person whispers something to the next person. That person does the same thing. By the time the words reach the last player, they have changed. This is what happened in the New World. The Golden Man was real, but the story turned into a golden city, a golden country, even seven golden cities. By Jimmie Angel's time, it had become a golden mountain.

Some men believed in El Dorado so much that they took bad risks. They wasted lives and a lot of money. These explorers wanted to find gold lying on the streets or to grab it from natives. When they didn't find that much, they lost hope. They didn't see that the New World was full of riches. It had new kinds of plants such as the potato, tomato, and pineapple. There were animals like bison,

llamas, golden eagles, and beavers.

Many explorers treated the natives very badly. This is one of the worst parts of the legend. Hundreds of thousands of native people died or were made slaves. They had lived there for thousands of years before the Europeans came. They built cities, roads, and canals. They invented pottery, the calendar,

and ways of working with metals like gold and silver. They traded and told each other stories. But they were no match for Europeans on horses carrying guns. The natives couldn't beat the Europeans in war, but they were clever. They tricked the Europeans with their stories.

Some good did come from these early searches. The American continents were mapped. Explorers made trails across the land for others to use. They wrote about huge bison, mighty rivers like the Amazon, and wonderful sights like the Grand Canyon and Angel Falls.

El Dorado has become part of our language. It still means something shiny and golden. Mostly, it now stands for an impossible dream that can't be reached.

Because of the legend, you can still find cities named El Dorado in California, Texas, Kansas, and all over South America. A famous American car was called the Eldorado. And the lost city still finds its way into many movies and video games. Legends help us share our beliefs in mighty people who seem special. They encourage people to paint, write books, and start new adventures. The stories we tell each other are very powerful. Even today, the legend of El Dorado is still a part of our lives.

AUTHOR'S NOTE

I found the search for El Dorado fascinating as I researched stories about it. I like gold as much as the next person, but I hadn't appreciated the force of greed behind the attempts to find El Dorado and the amazing power of a legend to drive people to seek it.

The most outrageous part of the search for El Dorado was how the natives were treated by Europeans. So many natives were killed, tortured, and enslaved that it's difficult to believe. But it did happen. The Europeans rode into cities and villages and grabbed what they wanted: not only treasure, but men, women, and children to work for them. It's a shameful chapter in the history of the Americas.

Much of South America became accessible to others by these gold seekers, and the southwestern United States was explored, too. Greed for gold sent so many people to California in 1849 that it became a state only one year later.

Once the Americas were opened up, millions of people from around the world moved in, mixed with the natives, and built new countries. Except for Brazil, where Portuguese is the official language, most South and Central Americans speak Spanish. English is the language of most North Americans, but native languages, French, and Spanish also remain. This mixing of Europeans, Asians, and natives in the Americas has resulted in whole new ways of life. This is the real result of the search for the El Dorado treasure.

TURN THE PAGE FOR MORE AMAZING FACTS!

THE STORY BEHIND THE STORY

THE SEARCH FOR EL DORADO

The legend of the lost city of gold has endured for thousands of years. Here are some of the most important events, people, and places you learned about.

c. 25,000 BCE	Hunting tribes live in the Americas.
1492–1493	Columbus makes his first voyage.
1493–1496	Columbus's second voyage visits Caribbean islands.
1498–1500	Columbus's third voyage visits Venezuela.
1502–1504	Columbus's fourth voyage visits Central America.
1519	Hernán Cortés conquers Mexico.

1532	Francisco Pizarro conquers Peru.
1540–1541	Francisco Vázquez de Coronado searches for gold in the present-day southwest United States.
1541	Gonzalo Pizarro tries to find El Dorado in South America.
1595	Sir Walter Raleigh makes his first trip to find El Dorado.
1609	Jamestown is founded.
1617	Sir Walter Raleigh makes his second trip.
1776	The Declaration of Independence is signed.
1849	Gold is discovered in California.
1933	Jimmie Angel flies over a huge, mysterious waterfall.
1937	Jimmie Angel and others visit the falls and look for gold.
1964	Venezuela declares Angel's plane a national treasure.
1970	Angel's plane is removed from the top of the mountain and repaired.

Keep reading to find out more about South America and what some of these places are like today!

COLOMBIA TODAY

Official name: Republic of Colombia
Capital: Bogotá
Official language: Spanish
Currency: Peso
Products: Petroleum, natural gas, gold, coal, iron, nickel, copper, emeralds, coffee, cut flowers, bananas
Native peoples: Muisca, Quimbaya, Tairona, and more

The Primary Cathedral of Bogotá

Fun fact! The Muisca people have lived for thousands of years in what is now Colombia. But what happened to their legendary gold? Some of it is in the Gold Museum in the capital, Bogotá. If you take a trip to the Gold Museum, you'll find one of the biggest collections of golden art in the world. There are rooms full of jewelry, figurines, masks, and more—all made by the native peoples of Colombia before the Spanish arrived.

Mask from the Gold Museum

MEXICO TODAY

Official name: United Mexican States
Capital: Mexico City
Official language: Spanish
Currency: Mexican peso
Products: Corn, wheat, soybeans, rice, beans, cotton, tobacco, chemicals, iron, steel, petroleum
Native peoples: Maya, Aztec, Toltec, and more

Metropolitan Cathedral and President's Palace in Mexico City

Fun fact! In the middle of the Mexican flag, there is a picture of an eagle with a snake and a cactus. The flag was designed to represent an important legend: Hundreds of years ago, the Aztec people wanted to build a new city. An Aztec god said that they could only build it where they found an eagle carrying a snake and landing on a cactus. That's a tough order! But after a long search, the Aztecs found this eagle and started building. Today, that city is the capital, Mexico City.

Close-up of an Aztec calendar

VENEZUELA TODAY

Official name: Bolivarian Republic of Venezuela
Capital: Caracas
Official language: Spanish
Currency: Bolívar
Products: Petroleum, steel, cement, aluminum, corn, sugar, rice, bananas, vegetables, coffee
Native peoples: Wayuu, Warao, Pemón, and more

Caracas city skyline

Fun fact! When Jimmie Angel found his waterfall in Venezuela, he also saw many strange plants and animals. In fact, Venezuela, Colombia, and Mexico are called *megadiverse* countries. They are home to many more different life-forms than most other countries. In Venezuela, you can find animal species like giant anteaters, three-toed sloths, Orinoco crocodiles, and capybaras—the world's largest rodent.

Three-toed sloth

BOOKS

Exploration and Conquest: The Americas After Columbus: 1500–1620 by Betsy and Giulio Maestro (New York: HarperCollins, 1994). Volume two in the Maestros' seven-volume American Story series, this lushly illustrated title (an ALA-ALSC Notable Children's Book) presents brief overviews of various explorers to the New World and the effects they had on native people. For ages 6 and up.

The Lost Colony of Roanoke by Jean Fritz, illustrated by Hudson Talbott (New York: G. P. Putnam's Sons, 2004). The story of Sir Walter Raleigh's Lost Colony—one of the most puzzling mysteries in American history—as told by an award-winning author-and-illustrator team. For ages 7 and up.

Sir Walter Ralegh and the Quest for El Dorado by Marc Aronson (New York: Clarion Books, 2000). This Robert F. Sibert Medal–winning biography explores Sir Walter's amazing accomplishments and dismal failures. For ages 12 and up.

What Was the Gold Rush? by Joan Holub, illustrated by Tim Tomkinson (New York: Grosset & Dunlap, 2013). Part of the popular What Was? series, this is an accessible look at the California Gold Rush of 1849, with black-and-white illustrations and photographs. For ages 8 and up.

Who Was First? Discovering the Americas by Russell Freedman (New York: Clarion Books, 2007). Written by a noted historian, this engaging book looks at who came to the Americas first, and why. A Bank Street College of Education Flora Stieglitz Straus Award winner. For ages 10 and up.

ABOUT THE AUTHOR

LOIS MINER HUEY is an archaeologist for the state of New York. She also writes nonfiction articles and books for kids, focusing on history and archaeology. Her most recent books are *Ick! Yuck! Eew! Our Gross American History* and *Forgotten Bones: Uncovering a Slave Cemetery*. Huey lives near Albany, New York, in a very old house with her archaeologist husband and three clean cats.

TOTALLY TRUE adventures!

CLIMBING EVEREST

Crack! An edge of ice split off and dropped into the deep, dark hole. Hillary fell. He tried to slow himself by jamming his boots into the icy wall.

"Tenzing!" he shouted. "Tenzing!"

In a flash, Tenzing plunged his ice ax into the snow. He wrapped his rope around the ax to hold it steady. Then he threw himself on the ground, to anchor the rope even more.

The rope tightened. Hillary jerked to a stop. He was fifteen feet down, far into the crack of ice. Bit by bit, he pulled himself up. His gloves were torn, and his body was bruised. But he was alive.

Excerpt copyright © 2015 by Gail Herman. Published by Random House Children's Books, a division of Penguin Random House LLC, New York.